YOUR KNOWLEDGE HAS VALUE

The Substantive and Procedural Rules Regarding Admissibility of Confessions

Datius Didace

Bibliographic information published by the German National Library:

The German National Library lists this publication in the National Bibliography; detailed bibliographic data are available on the Internet at http://dnb.dnb.de.

ISBN: 9783346636188
This book is also available as an ebook.

Print and binding: Books on Demand GmbH, Norderstedt, Germany
Printed on acid-free paper from responsible sources.

The present work has been carefully prepared. Nevertheless, authors and publishers do not incur liability for the correctness of information, notes, links and advice as well as any printing errors.

GRIN web shop: https://www.grin.com/document/1192537

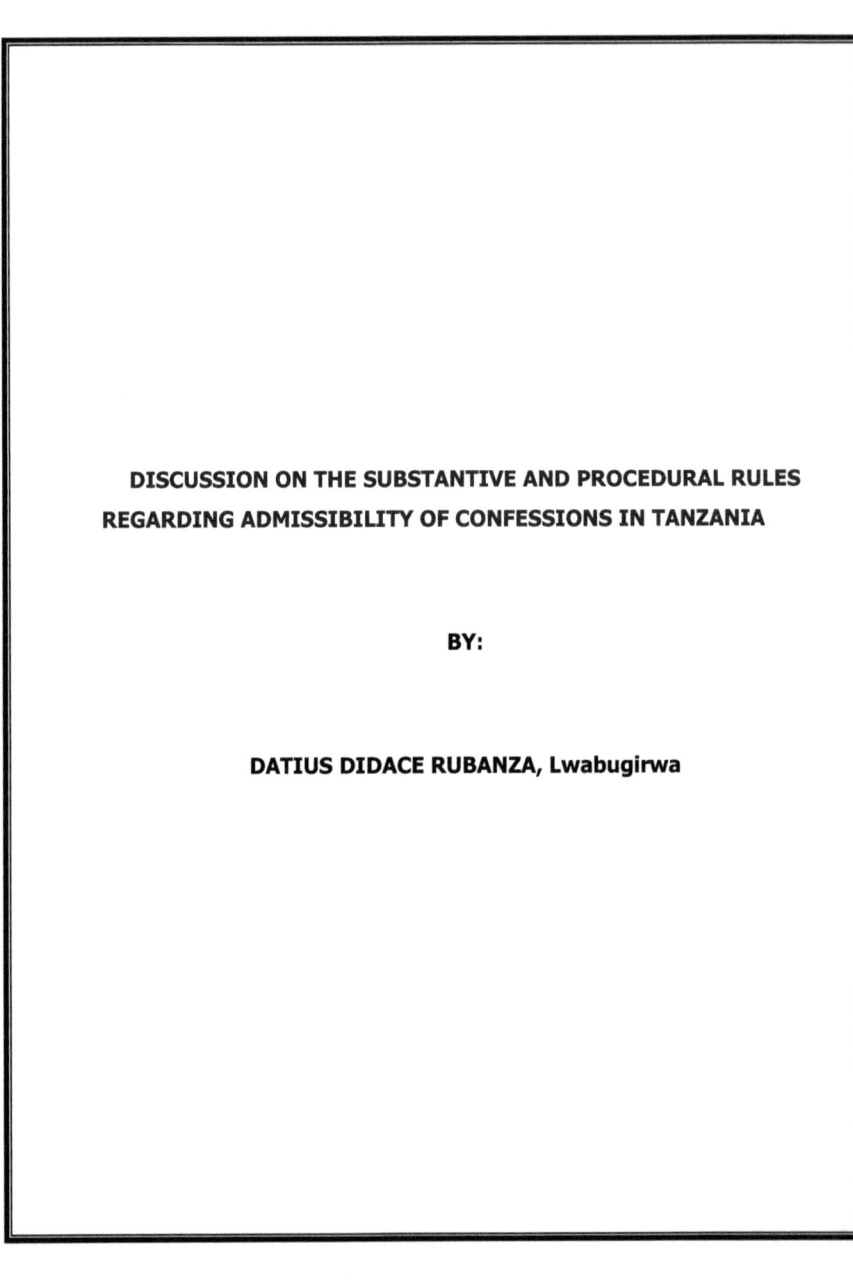

DISCUSSION ON THE SUBSTANTIVE AND PROCEDURAL RULES
REGARDING ADMISSIBILITY OF CONFESSIONS IN TANZANIA

BY:

DATIUS DIDACE RUBANZA, Lwabugirwa

TABLE OF CONTENTS

1.0 INTRODUCTION

Admissions and confessions are these statements are admissible on the strength that admissible *as exceptions to the rule against hearsay evidence.* They are based on the principle that no person can make statement against his own interest unless it is true.

The general rule in both civil and criminal cases is that any relevant statement made by a party is evidence against him. In civil cases, for instance, statements made out of court by a party to the proceedings or by a person connected with him by any of the relationships are admissible in evidence against but not usually in favor of such a party. In regarding to the law of Evidence Act[1] which covers different aspects including both substantive and procedural rules, has attributed it a substantive law at the same time it's a procedural law. Therefore taking Confession, the Court of Appeal has often provided information on how our Judges (Justice of Peace) are required to take confession or confession of wrongdoing. Unfortunately, these instructions have been disregarded and thus have been the source of many dismissal appeals by this Court.

Factors to consider are clearly stated in the case of **Hatibu Gandhi & Others v. Republic**[2] and **Petro Teophan vs The Republic**[3]. It will be better if they were read intensively and educate judges in courts of law. Aggrieved with those Court of appeal decisions, the judges should go through the book called **"A Guide for Justice of the Peace"**[4].To expedite the implementation of these resolutions herein, we have explained the whole substantive and procedure for taking a confession statement.

1.1 SCOPE OF THE QUESTION

The question requires us to discuss about the Substantive and Procedural Rules regarding admissibility of either Confessions or Admissions. In respect the instruction of the question, herein we shall deal with the term Confession. In our discussion, we shall

---

[1] Cap 6 RE 2019
[2] [1996] T.L.R.12
[3] Criminal Appeal No. 58 of 2012 (unreported)
[4] Judiciary of Tanzania, A Handbook For Magistrates In The Primary Courts: Published By The Judiciary of Tanzania With The Support of The World Bank, January 2019. (Page 116-131)

first begin with the meaning of Law of Evidence together with Substantive rules and Procedural rules, and the conceptualization of Confession, Thereafter, we are going to discuss the Substantive and Procedural Rules regarding admissibility of Confession, Additionally, the general rule as to the admissibility confession cautioned statement and extra judicial statement

1.2 LAW OF EVIDENCE

The law of evidence is that branch of the law that regulates production and admissibility of evidence in judicial and other proceedings.

1.2.1 Substantive rules

Stipulate *rights* and *duties* of individuals. Also, when you talk about substantive rules you are talking about a law that has to provide things in rest or a law that has to provide things that are. **For example**; if it is a civil law that provides rights and obligation, if it is a criminal law that provides of their rights and punishment, if it is a principle then the law that provides for is precedents conditional for is something to be accepted.The Tanzania Evidence Act provides for situations in which a confession can lawfully be made;

1.2.2 Procedural rules or adjectival law

Consists of rules that are used toenforce private or public duties and the public discipline, writs, process,trials, judgments, executions, and so forth.Thus, the Law of Evidence belongs to theadjective/adjectival or procedural law

2.0 CONCEPTUALIZATION OF CONFESSION

The term confession has been defined by various jurists[5]and even some judicial decisions have taken their consideration in defining this term. **Ratanlal vs. R**[6]. Defines this term to mean;

> *"An admission made at any time by a person charged with a crime, stating or suggesting the inference that he committed that crime."*

Stephen[7]. Defines this term confession to mean;

> *"An admission made by a person charged with a crime stating or suggesting the inference that he committed that crime"*

From the above two meanings of the term confession it can be drawn an observation that the term confession has its basis on criminal matters other than in civil matters and that it can be stating or even drawing an inference to the commission of a crime.

Also, the term confession has been defined under **Section 3 (1)** of the Evidence Act[8]. In **DPP v ACP Abdallah Zombe & Others**[9], quoted definitions from; The *Oxford Advanced Learners Dictionary*: "Say or admit, often formally that one has done wrong, committed a crime."*Black Law Dictionary*: "Is acknowledgment in express words by the accused in criminal case of the truth of the main fact charged or of some essential part of it[10]."So, in this context a confession is a voluntary admission of guilty to an offence.

In the case of **Mathei Fidoline Haule v R**[11], the Court of Appeal of Tanzania stated that: a confession within the context of criminal law is one which admits in terms the offence charged. It is one which admits all the essential elements or ingredients of the

---

[5] For instance in Heydon, J.D (1991) **Evidence: Cases and Materials**, 3rdEdn, at p.173 says that; "Generally speaking, a confession is a statement by the accused in which he admits committed an offence, or admits some fact that goes to show he committed an offence"

[6] Ratanlal, R &D.K.Thakore, (2004) **The Law of Evidence**, 21stEdn, p.164

[7]As cited in Phipson, S.L (1982) **Phipson on Evidence**, p.674

[8] Cap 6 R.E 2019

[9] Criminal Appeal No. 358 of 2013 (Unreported) CA

[10] M.N. Howard, et al (1990) **Phipson on Evidence**, 14th Edition p 674. The same is found in Chandra chund and Manohar **op cit**p 93, where the author added that the term confession is a statement which either admits in terms of the offence or at any rate substantially all the facts which constitutes theoffence.

[11] [1992] TLR 148 at 151

offence. An admission of one or only some of the ingredients of the offence is not sufficient.

Furthermore, the case of **R v Kifungu Nsurupia**[12] it was stated that the term confession connotes an unequivocal admission of having committed an act which in law amounts to a crime. In the case of **R v Bampamiyki**[13] the court stated that for the statement to amount to a confession it must contain all the ingredients of the crime with which the accused person is charged so that the accused could be properly convicted on his own plea.

Also the word confession has been defined in the case of **Mwiroma v R**[14], the court held that a statement admitting shortage of funds in a case of theft constitutes an admission not a confession. And in the case of **Songwe Ngedeleie v R**[15], judge Seat on said: "A *confession* is" a direct acknowledgement of guilt on the part of the accused...an admission... is a statement by theaccused, direct or implied of facts pertinent to the issue and tending, in connection with *proof* of other facts, to prove his guilt, but of itself is insufficient to authorize a conviction".

However, in the case of **Michael John @Mtei v. R**[16], it was stated that in a confession the prosecution has to prove: (i) the accused by his conduct or words made a statement, and (ii) the statement or conduct amounting to a confession was freely and voluntarily made. Again, in **Rhino Migere v. R**[17], the case envisages the statement to qualify for a confession it must contain the admission of all the ingredients of the offence charged as provided for under **section 3(c)** of the Evidence Act."

Further, in **Gervas Kilongozi vs. R**[18] the appellant was charged and convicted with murder. The trial court based the conviction on a confession that the appellant made to

---

[12] [1941] 8 EACA 89
[13] [1957] EA 473
[14] (1968) HCD n. 181
[15] (1968) HCD 178
[16] Criminal Appeal No.202 of 2012, CAT (unreported)
[17] Criminal Appeal No.122 of 2002, CAT (unreported)
[18] [1994] TLR 39 CA

4

a police officer whose rank is not shown on the evidence. On appeal the conviction on confession was challenged as being on inadmissible evidence.It was undisputed that there was nothing on record to show that the police officer to whom the appellant made the confession was of the rank required. It was held that, "*Confession was inadmissible in evidence and that the case was not proved beyond reasonable doubt*". For these reasons appeal allowed.

As far as generally understood, a confession is an acknowledgement in express terms by a party in a criminal case of his guilt. Thus defined, a confession implies an admission of every essential element necessary to establish the crime with which the defendant is charged.

2.1 The Types of Confession
Hereunder are two types of confessions which are relevant and admissible

2.1.1 Judicial confession
In this type the accused person admits the commission of the crime. This confession is taken by the magistrate during the preliminary examination taken in writing before the trial began[19]. It should be noted that in the plea of guilty the accused is allowed to change his plea because once the plea is entered, the court will convict the accused person.It is judicial when made before a magistrate in the course of legalproceeding.

2.1.2 Extrajudicial confession
This refers to confessions made before the commencement of a trial either to a police officer or justice of peace, the onus of proving that it was voluntary lies to the prosecution.In addition, an extra judicial confession freely and voluntarily made may be proved as against that person[20]. An extra judicial confession can be accepted without corroboration if other evidence inspires confidence.An extra judicial confession by its

---

[19]   https://blog.ipleaders.in/important-pointers-you-must-know-about-admissibility-of-confessions/#Introduction (Accessed on 13th may, 2021)
[20] Mapunda B.T., (2004). **Evidence Part one, Two & Three**, 1st Ed., The Open University of Tanzania, Dar es Salaam

very nature is rather a weak type of evidence and requires appreciation with a great deal of care and caution[21].

3.0 THE SUBSTANTIVE RULES REGARDING ADMISSIBILITY OF CONFESSION

It is in general immaterial to whom a voluntary confession has been made. Thus, a confession made to a person in authority is admissible, if not induced by him,while one induced by, though not made to him will be rejected. So statements made, or letters written, when in custody, by the accused to the prosecutor,or to outside friends,where the letter was written after trial and received on appeal, or to his wife, or statements made by the prisoner to his wife or even to himself,or confidences to a fellow prisoneroverheard by the police, or statements to solicitor, are admissible, if independently proved.

For the foregoing reason, we hereby explain the substantive rules regarding admissibility of confession:

3.1 Confession must be made to an authorized person

Section 27 (1) and Section 28 of the Evidence Act[22], which provides the list of persons, who can receive confession to include police officer, justice of peace and magistrates respectively. Hence the confession made to other person than the above, will be invalid under the law.In the case of **Shihobe Seni and Another v Republic[23]**, the appellants were said to have made confessions that they later repudiated. Some of the confessions were made to the village chairman. The court held a view that a village chairman is a person in authority under section 27(3) of the Evidence Act and so a confession made to him is involuntary if the Court believes that it was not induced by any threat, promise or other prejudice. There is not a thread of doubt that the confessions to the village chairman were not induced by threat, promise or other prejudice

---

[21] Best, W.M,.(1911). **The Principles of the Law of Evidence**. London: Sweet & Maxwell.
[22] Cap 6, R.E 2019
[23] [1992] TLR 330 (CA)

3.2 Confession will be the valid if made freely and voluntarily

Voluntariness of a confession is a key component in the admissibility of a confession[24].A confession is not voluntarily made if it was induced by threat, promise or other prejudice held by the police or any other person in authority. Voluntariness of the confession is provided under Section 27 of The Evidence Act.

The provision of Section 29 of TEA[25] is to the effect that "No confession which is tendered in evidence shall be rejected on the ground that a promise or threat has been held out to, the person confessing unless the court is of the opinion that the inducement was made in such circumstances and was of such a nature as was likely to cause an untrue admission of guilt to be made"The above provision is reflected in the case of **Josephat Somisha Maziku v R[26],** the High Court of Tanzania stated that; While it is trite law, that the condition precedent for the admissibility of the confession, is its voluntariness, the said confession is not automatically inadmissible, simply because it resulted from threats, or promise; it is inadmissible, only if the inducement or threat, was of such a nature as was likely to cause an untrue admission of guilt.

Also, in the case of **Njuguna and Another vs. R[27]**it was stated that, *"It was incumbent upon the prosecution to prove that the confession was voluntarily made and was not obtained by improper or unlawful questioning or other methods."*

Onus of proving if the confession was voluntarily made lies to the prosecution side, as per Section 27 (2) of TEA. However, it is the duty of the court to examine with close care and attention all the circumstances in which the confession was obtained. There are several cases which exemplify this; in **Diamon s/o Malakela @ Maunganya v. R[28],**where the court held that at this juncture I must point out that Section 27(2) the onus of proving that any confession made by an accused person was voluntarily made

---

[24] Peter Murphy, (1992). **A practical Approach to Evidence**, 4[th]Ed, Blackstone Press Ltd, London
[25] Tanzania Evidence Act, Cap 6 R.E 2019
[26][1992]TLR 227 at 230,
[27] [1952] 2 EACA 311
[28] Criminal Appeal No.205 of 2005, CAT (unreported)

by him shall lie on the prosecution., Section 28[29]. A confession which is freely and voluntarily made by a person accused of an offence in the immediate presence of a magistrate as defined in the Magistrates' Courts Act, or a justice of the peace under that Act, may be proved as against that person.

The court has to examine so as to adhere the confession that was voluntarily made, if such confession was made out of inducement as per Section 27 (3)[30]. The term inducement has two main meanings and such are; *"fear of prejudice"* or *"hope of advantage"*.

Section 27 (3) of the Evidence Act provides that the confession should be induced by any threat, promise or any other prejudice. However, the inducement requires actual state of the accused mind and other factors.

In the case of **DPP vs. Ping Lin[31]**, it was held that, *"The test depends on the actual effect on the accused mind. Subjective considerations are also relevant where the inducement proceeds from a person who is in authority. However, the inducement must not be too vague. It must point to some consequences."*

However, Section 29 of the Tanzania Evidence Act[32] provides for the exceptions of the voluntariness. Inducement is not in itself sufficient reason to reject confession. Such confession can only be rejected if it was made in such circumstances and in such nature which likely to cause untrue admission, for example in the case of **Brasius Maona and Gaitan Mgao v. R[33]**, it was held that Once torture has been established courts should be cautious in admitting such statements in evidence even under the provisions of section 29 of the Evidence Act[34], which in our considered opinion was not meant to be invoked in situations where inducement involved is torture.

---

[29] [Cap 6 R.E 2019]
[30] Tanzania Evidence Act, Cap 6, R.E 2019
[31] (1976) AC 574
[32] Cap 6 R.E 2019
[33] Criminal Appeal No.215 of 1992, CAT (unreported)
[34] Cap 6 R.E 2019

In the case of **Josephat Somisha Maziku vs. Republic[35]**, In this case the court stated inter alia that, While it is trite law that the condition precedent for the admissibility of a confession is its voluntariness, a confession is not automatically inadmissible simply because it resulted from threats or promise, it is inadmissible only if the inducement or threat was of such a nature as was likely to cause an untrue admission of guilt[36].

3.3 Confession it must be made by an accused person himself.

The ingredient which makes the confession to be valid is that it must be made by an accused person himself; however, there is the situation whereby the accused make the confession against his co-accused. However no person can be convicted solely on the basis of the confession of co-accused. In order for a confession of co-accused to be admitted there are conditions to be fulfilled.This was stressed in the case of **Asia Iddi vs. R[37]**, A confession of an offence other than the one with which the accused is charged is deemed to be a confession for the purpose of that offence. Example.A is accused of murder but he admits to manslaughter. The confession to manslaughter will be admissible to prove manslaughter. It will however not be admissible to prove murder.

In the case of **Bampamiyki s/o Buhile v. R[38],** the accused had been charged with murder, whereby a house had been burnt down and two people died in the fire. The accused made a confession to a police officer that he had burnt the house. The Court of Appeal held that the confession was inadmissible in the murder charge.

Thus, generally a confession can be made to any person provided that it is made voluntarily and it is true.

---

[35] [1992] TLR 227 (HC)
[36] J. L. Ingram, (2012). **Criminal Evidence,** Anderson Publishing, Elsevier
[37] [1989] TLR 174 HC
[38] (1957) EA 473

4.0 THE PROCEDURAL RULES REGARDING THE ADMISSIBILITY OF CONFESSIONS.

Hereunder are the procedural rules regarding admissibility of confessions, When it comes to Procedural requirements how should it be taken here, I will start by explaining caution statement because someone can confess fire caution statement, how a caution statement should be taken?, what if the accused person has been admitted to the police officer when it comes to the court he has a denial here there are many issues like, repudiated and retracted confession and what if the accused said the confession was retracted or repudiated, that he can say, I have never made such a confession now procedural, so substantive rules, of course, is based on more laws in terms of status, evidence act but on procedural, there are cases laws that help in the procedure, for example, the issue of trial within the trial or inquiry.

4.1 Special powers of Justices assigned to District Court- houses

Consequently, **Section 57** Magistrate Court Act[39], A justice assigned to a District Court house may take and record the confessions of persons in the custody of the police. A prisoner wishing to make a statement may be brought to the office of a justice under police escort and usually bearing a letter from the Officer-in- Charge, Police, to the effect that the accused, who is under arrest in connection with an alleged offence, wishes to make a voluntary statement to a magistrate/ Justice[40].

4.2 Cautioned Statement

The Cautioned Statements, the law governing in Tanzania are the **Evidence Act[41]** and the **Criminal Procedure Act[42]** as shown hereunder; According to **Section 10 (3), section 57** which read together with **Section 58 of The Criminal Procedure Act[43]**

---

[39] Cap 11 R.E 2019
[40] Judiciary of Tanzania, **A Hand book For Magistrates in the Primary Courts:** Published by the Judiciary of Tanzania with the Support of The World Bank, January 2019. (Page 116-131)
[41] [Cap 6 RE 2019]
[42] [Cap 20 R.E 2019]
[43] Ibid

proves for admissibility of confession made by an accused person to the police officer that is when a police officer makes an investigation, or interview to person, must record the statement in full language used unless it in all circumstances impracticable to do so and emphasis to made a cautioned statement to a person before he made the confession.

In the case of **Athuman Rashid vs. The Republic[44]**, provide that: (1) the provisions of **section 57** of the Criminal Procedure Act, seek to ensure that the statements allegedly made to the police by suspects are voluntary and free from error. (2) Where a cautioned statement is objected to for want of a certificate as required by sub-section (3) of the Act, the court should ascertain on the voluntariness and correctness of the statement, usually by holding a trial within a trial. If the court is satisfied that the statement was made voluntarily and was recorded correctly it should proceed to admit it in evidence, but if it is not so satisfied then it should accordingly hold it inadmissible. (3) It is not mandatory for the question and answer style to be used. **Section 57(2) (a)** of the Act[45] speaks of "so far as it is practicable to do so" suggesting that where it is impracticable one may dispense with that style.

Also under **section 27(1)** of The Evidence Act[46], provides for the same admissibility of confession of cautioned statement that is a confession voluntarily made to a police by a person accused of an offence may be proved against that person, police officer must be of or above the rank of corporal, as prescribed by thee law otherwise the evidence will be inadmissible, this is supported in the case of **Gervas Kilongozi vs. R[47]**, in this case it was held that the confession was inadmissible in evidence and that case was not proven beyond reasonable doubt due to the failure to show the rank of a police officer.

---

[44] Criminal Appeal No.138 of 1994, CAT (unreported)
[45] Criminal Procedure Act, Cap 20 R.E 2019
[46] [CAP 6 R.E 2002]
[47] [1994] TLR 39

Therefore, Caution is a warning to a person that his answer to the questions may be used in evidence.[48], **Cautioned statement** are statement made by a person officer to a person suspected to an offence to be cautioned before any question put to him for the purpose of obtaining evidence which may be given to a court in a prosecution, such confession is admissible whether it was made before the arrest or after arrest in case of a juvenile, must be cautioned in the presence of his guardian and unsound mind or handicapped person must be interpreted till understood the matter.

Cautioned statements are given in the case of **Balbisain Josh.**[49], that whether that police takes a statements of the accused person he must caution him by saying that you're not obliged to say anything unless you wish to do so, but what you say may be put in writing and given in evidence.

4.3   Confession is Extrajudicial Statement

When made by the accused person elsewhere other than before the court, such a statement made under the person with authority or to the justice e of peace.The term embraced not only express confession of a crime but also those admission and acts of the accused from which guilt may be implied. It is sufficient to warrant a conviction[50].

On the other hand the law governing the admissibility of confession on extra-judicial statements is based on the Magistrate's Court Act[51] and The Evidence Act.According to **Section 51** and **57** and **59** of **The Magistrate's Court Act**[52] provides that officer of district, town, municipal or city council are justice of peace who has assigned the power to hear, take and record the confession of a person in custody of a police and such confession in admissible[53]. It further stated under **Section 28** of

---

[48] Osborn's Concise Law Dictionary, 18th Edition, at Page 63.
[49] (1951) 18 EA CA 208
[50] Mapunda B.T., (2004). **Evidence Part one, Two & Three**, 1st Ed., The Open University of Tanzania, Dar es Salaam
[51] Cap 11 R.E 2019
[52] Ibid
[53] Sarkar, P.I.C. & Sarkar,(1981). **S. Sarkar's Law of Evidence**, Calcutta, S.C. Sarkar & Sons (Private) Ltd.

The Evidence Act[54] that a confession which is freely and voluntarily made by a person accused of an offence in presence of the magistrate or justice of the peace is admissible as an extrajudicial statement[55].

As well, in the case of **Nyeura Patrick vs. the Republic[56]**, in this case **Mmilla, J.A.,**

Held that, *(i) A confession voluntarily made by accused to a police officer of above the rank of corporals is admissible in evidence. However, in order for such statement to be admitted, it must be established that it was made voluntarily. In terms of section 27(2) of the Evidence Act[57], the onus of proving voluntariness lies on the prosecution. It is the court which is charged with the duty to determine voluntariness or otherwise of such statement in any inquiry to be conducted by it. (ii) If an objection is made after the trial has informed the accused of his right to say something in connection with the alleged confession the trial court must stop everything and proceed to conduct an inquiry* **(or a trial within trial)** *into voluntariness or not of the alleged confession such inquiry should be conducted before the confession is admitted in evidence.*

(iii) The trial within trial is of course, one designed to cater for accused's right to a fair trial in order to ensure that questions of admissibility and of guilt are distinguishable from each other and decided separately. If it may be established after trial within trial that the statement is involuntary the court is duty bound to reject such evidence.

(iii) Where it may be established that the trial court did not hold a trial within trial after an objection was made against admissibility of the said statement, there is no better option for the court but to make an order expunging that statement.

---

[54] [CAP 6 R.E 2019]
[55] **Judiciary of Tanzania.**, A Handbook For Magistrates in The Primary Courts:Published: By The Judiciary of Tanzania With The Support of The World Bank, January,2019
[56] Criminal Appeal No. 73 of 2013: Court of Appeal of Tanzania at Mwanza (Unreported).
[57] Cap 6 of R.E, 2019

In addition to that, in the case of **Hatibu Gandhi & Others vs. R[58]**, In this case the court also made four important remarks, (i) In deciding whether a magistrate's failure to comply fully with the Chief Justice's Instructions renders **extra-judicial statements** inadmissible, the question is whether apart from any such non-compliance, other circumstances suggest that the statements were made involuntarily. (ii) A conviction on a retracted uncorroborated confession is competent if the court warns itself of the danger of acting upon such a confession and is fully satisfied that such confession cannot but be true. (iii) A retracted uncorroborated confession, if truthful, can corroborate other evidence against the confessor. (iv) Incriminating statements made at a trial within the trial are admissible at the main trial and can be used against their maker at the main trial.

It was also observed, in the case of **Petro Teophan vs. The Republic[59]**, in this case the Court went on: The Justice of the Peace ought to observe, *inter alia,* the following:

(i) The time and date of his arrest,

(ii) The place he was arrested,

(iii) The place he slept before the date he was brought to him,

(iv) Whether any person by threat or promise or violence he has persuaded him to give the statement.

(v) Whether he really wishes to make the statement on his own free will. And

(vi) That if he makes a statement the same may be used as evidence against him.

It should be remembered that, A **Guide of Justice of Peace** issued by Chief Justice reviling how Justice of Peace must record Extra judicial Statement of accused person, and **"A Guide for Justice of Peace"** came into force on 1 July, 1964 the date when the Magistrate Court Act, 1963 came into force. Though the Magistrate Court Act of 1963, was repealed and replaced by the current Magistrate Court Act[60], by virtue

---

[58] [1996] TLR 12
[59] Criminal Appeal No. 58 of 2012 (unreported)
[60] Magistrate Court Act, Cap 11 R.E 2019

of saving provisions as contained in Section 72(3) of the current Magistrate Court Act, those regulations are taken to have been made under the current Magistrate Court Act[61].

So, *"A Guide for Justice of Peace"* are part and parcel of the laws of this Country. Whereas the case of **Japhet Thadei Msigwa v. The Republic[62]**, the Court observed:

So, when Justices of the Peace are recording confessions of persons in the custody of the police, they must follow the Chief Justice's Instructions to the letter. The section is couched in mandatory terms. "

5.0 THE GENERAL RULE AS TO THE ADMISSIBILITY CONFESSION CAUTIONED STATEMENT AND EXTRA JUDICIAL STATEMENT

The law provides that such statement must be free from threats, promise or other prejudice held out by a police officer to whom it was made or by any member of the police force or by any other person in authority. However the test is objective in the fact that not every inducement has the effect of making confession involuntary.

In the case of **Kuruma s/o Kanin v. R[63]**, Lord Goddard, C.J. stated that: It is right.., that the rule with regard to the admission of confession, whether it be regarded as an exception to the general rule or not, is a rule of law which their Lordships are not qualifying in any degree whatsoever. *The rule is that a confession can only be admitted if it is voluntary and therefore, one obtained by threats or promises held out by a person in authority is not to be admitted.*

Voluntaries of a confession is a key component in the admissibility of any confession, therefore as a general rule a confession must be freely and voluntarily made as it is provided under **section 27** and **section 28** of **The Evidence Act[64]**, that a confession voluntarily made to a police or justice of peace are admissible and shall be held to be involuntary if the court believes that it was induced by any threat, promise or other

---

[61] Section 57(1)(a) and section 59 of Magistarte Court Act, Cap 11 R.E 2019
[62] Criminal Appeal No. 367 of 2008, CAT (unreported)
[63] [1955] 1 All E.R. 236
[64] Cap 6 R.E 2019

prejudice held out by the police officer or any other person in authority, this was supported in the case of **Shihobe Seni and Another vs R**[65] in this case thee court held a village chairman is person with authority under section 27(3) of The Evidence Act and therefore the confession was admissible as there were not induced by threat, promise or other prejudice[66].

5.1 Exception to the General Ruleas to the Admissibility Confession Cautioned Statement and Extra Judicial Statement

There are other circumstances in which not every inducement has the effect on confession involuntary and that confession accused by induced, threat or promise can be admissible unless such inducement was likely to cause untrue admission of guilt of a person, this is provided under **section 29** read together with **section 30** of **The Evidence Act**[67]which states that confession made after the removal of impression caused by inducement, threat, or promise need not be rejected ,this was held in the case of **Josephat Somisha Maziku vs R**[68]. When confession leading to the discovery of a new thing relates to the fact in issue is relevant as it was held in the case of **John Peter Shao vs R**[69], the court held that since an accused mentioned things stolen that hidden somewhere is admissible.

It is further argued that, a confession is not just reject able, because threats have been made. It is for the prosecution to prove voluntariness of the confession, and once a threat has been shown to have been made, the Court may presume, that it induced the confession, until the prosecution proves, that there was no causal connection,

---

[65] [1992] TLR 330
[66] C. Nemeth,(2012). **Law and Evidence**: A Primer for Criminal Justice, Criminology, Law and Legal Studies, Learning, London
[67] Cap 6 R.E 2019
[68] [1992] TLR 227
[69] [1998] TLR 198

So that where you have threats, and a confession far apart, without causal connection, and no chance of such threats inducing confession, such confession should be taken to be free of inducement voluntary, and admissible[70].

The confession made as a result of a promise of secrecy or deception regardless he was not warned that he was not bound to make such confession is relevant and admissible under **section 32 of The Evidence Act,** the court may reflect to admit such confession made voluntary or rendered unfair to a person this was stated in the case **Nayinda vs R[71].**

In the case of **Deo kinan v R[72],** The police planted a friend of the accused in the same cell with the accused, to which the accused confessed the crime. The friend then conveyed this to the police. The court held that this confession was admissible as it was not made after an inducement by a person in authority. Also in the case of **Naginda s/o Batungwa v R[73],** the Court however held that nothing in the section above negated the discretion of the judge to refuse to admit a statement when he thought that it was not voluntary.

The other important principle discussed under **Section 33** of The Evidence Act[74] provides that confession against co-accused when one of them confess by incriminating the other such confession will be admissible with certain caution, as it was supported in the case of *Asia Iddi vs R*[75] the court held that the evidence of a person who has an interest to serve needs corroborated.

5.2 The Criticism Regarding to Admissibility of Confessions

The admissibility of confession both cautioned statement and extra judicial statement is not final and conclusive to convict a person due to the fact that a person accused of

---

[70] Mapunda B.T., (2004). **Evidence Part one, Two & Three**, 1st Ed., The Open University of Tanzania, Dar es Salaam
[71](1959) EA 688
[72] (1969) 1 AC 20
[73] (1959) EA,
[74][CAP 6 R.E 2019]
[75] [1989] TLR 174

an offence is brought before the court of law must be asked whether he disputes the a admissibility of confession.

Once he repudiated or retracted a confession the court must conduct a trial within a trial in order to determine its voluntaries or admissibility and is where the prosecution side need to prove such confession beyond reasonable doubt[76], and when the court satisfies that a retracted or denied confession cannot support a conviction unless corroborated, as supported in the case of *Jackson s/o Mwakatoka and 2 others vs R*[77] which states that as a matter of prudence corroboration is important any retracted or repudiated.

5.3   Repudiated and Retracted Confession

In some instances, confession may be retracted or repudiated.

A retracted confession occurs where the accused admits that he or she has made the confession and then denies the truth to what is stated therein.

Repudiated confession is one which the accused person avers that he never made.in the case of repudiated or denied confession, provided that the court was satisfied that the accused did in fact made the confession, it would be reasonable to infer that it was denied because of its truth and corroboration would not normally be necessary.

This rule however has been modified from time to time and is now settled that there may be circumstances in which corroboration is not necessary. In **Tuwamoi v. Uganda[78]**, held that:

"The present rule then as applied in East Africa, in regard to a retracted confession, is that as a matter of practice or prudence the trial court should direct itself that it is dangerous to act upon a statement which has been retracted in the absence of corroboration in some material particular, but that the court might do so if it is fully satisfied in the circumstances of the case that the confession must be true."

---

[76] Morris, H.F (1968). **Evidence in East Africa**: Sweet & Maxwell, African University Press, Lagos, Nigeria.
[77] [1990] TLR 17
[78] [1967] E.A. 84

5.4 PRINCIPLES TO FOLLOW WHERE THERE IS A DANGER TO ACT UPON REPUDIATED OR RETRACTED CONFESSION

Hereunder are the principles to follow where there is a danger to act upon repudiated or retracted confession.

5.4.1 Corroboration

This means that, if there is an independent piece of evidence connecting the confessor with the offence alleged, the court can convict[79]. This principle was emphasized by the court of appeal of Tanzania in the case of **Tadei Mlomo and others vs. R**[80], the court said, "*There was corroborative evidence to support the conviction of the third appellant on the basis of the repudiated confession of his co-accused.*"

In this case we have learned that, in the case where more than one person are jointly charged, the corroborative evidence incriminating one accused can be used as against the remaining accused person. This means either way court procedures remain the same where rights of accused persons are not prejudiced.

5.4.2 Trial within the Trial

It is now a trite law as demonstrated above that, a court may convict on a retracted or repudiated confession even without corroboration, though such confession must be received with great cautions. But before the inference is drawn and taking in regard all circumstances of the case, the court find it unsafe to continue with the proceedings, it can hold trial within a trial[81].

This argument was discussed in the case of **M'murairi s/o Karegwa vs. R**[82], where the court emphasized that, where the trial court fails to hold trial within a trial as a result of which the accused is forced to give evidence generally and has thereby been

---

[79]Mapunda B.T., (2004). **Evidence Part one, Two & Three**, 1 st Ed., The Open University of Tanzania, Dar es Salaam
[80] (1995) TLR 187
[81] Sarkar, M. C., (1983), Sarkar's Law of Evidence, 14thedtn., Vol.1, p. 395
[82](1954) 21 EACA 262

prejudiced, the effect may be that, not only can not the disputed statement not to be looked at, but that the conviction cannot stand.

To make more clearly however, in the case of **John Peter Shayo and Others vs. R**[83], the Court of Appeal of Tanzania had made clarification on how trial within trial should be exercised. The court said inter alia that, *"A trial within trial is a practice which only obtains in a criminal trial held by the High Court where a Judge sits with assessors."*It appears that, this practice is not statutorily provided but rather had been developed through case law. *"Trial within trial will be conducted on the grounds which would appear to the court reasonable. It shows that the word 'appears' imports judicial discretion. It means that the court has to decide the preliminary question of admissibility or otherwise of the confession on a consideration of the evidence and surrounding circumstances.*The court has to determine the sufficiency of the inducement, threat or promise as affording grounds reasonable to conduct trial within a trial."*[84]

---

[83] (1998) TLR 198
[84] Rantalal&Dhirajlal, (2019). The Law of Evidence. Lexis Nexis, Publishers.

6.0   SUMMARY AND CONCLUSION

This work has been an enquiry into the substantive and procedural rules regarding admissibility of Confessions. Confession it'sa statement made by an accused person who is sought to be proved against him in criminal proceeding establishes the commission of offence by him.

What I have endeavored to state, Confession as substantive evidence has high probative value and is appreciated the most by court of law. Conviction can be based solely on the basis of confession if its voluntariness and reliability is undoubted. Confession carries a vehement force in itself and can drive the whole proceeding in a particular direction therefore; the seriousness attached with confession must not be undermined. It must be observed with a lot of caution and circumspection so as to expunge even slight chances of error. The confession must always be an outcome of conscience burdened with guilt and contrition.

On the other hand, this work has argued that it is important to recognize that some of the rules and principles which have sometimes been underlying reason for making the confession must always be colored with repentance and remorse and not with oppression or influence. Therefore, it becomes indispensable to ensure the truthfulness and voluntariness of confession.

BIBLIOGRAPHY

STATUES

Tanzania Evidence Act [Cap.6 R.E 2019]

The Criminal Procedure Act [Cap.20 R.E 2019]

The Magistrate Court Act [Cap.11 R.E 2019]

CASES

Asia Iddi vs R [1989] TLR 174

Athuman Rashid vs Republic, Criminal Appeal No.138 of 1994: Court of Appeal of Tanzania, (unreported)

DPP v ACP Abdallah Zombe& Others, Criminal Appeal No. 358 of 2013: Court of Appeal at Dar es Salaam (Unreported)

Gervas Kilongozi vs R, [1994] TLR 39 CA

Hatibu Gandhi & Others v R [1996] TLR 12

Jackson s/o Mwakatoka and 2 others vs R [1990] TLR 17

Japhet Thadei Msigwa v. Republic, Criminal Appeal No. 367 of 2008 (unreported)

John Peter Shayo and Others vs. R(1998) TLR 198

Josephat Somisha Maziku vs R [1992] TLR 227

Mathei Fidoline Haule v Republic (1992) TLR 148 CA

Michael John @Mtei v. R, Criminal Appeal No.202 of 2012; Court of Appeal at Dar es Salaam, (unreported)

Nyeura Patrick vs Republic, Criminal Appeal No. 73 of 2013: Court of Appeal of Tanzania at Mwanza, (Unreported).

Petro Teophanv. Republic, Criminal Appeal No. 58 of 2012: Court of Appeal of Tanzania at Dodoma (Unreported).

Rhino Migere v. R, Criminal Appeal No.122 of 2002 (unreported)

Shihobe Seni and Another v Republic [1992] TLR 330 (CA)

Tadei Mlomo and others vs. R (1995) TLR 187

BOOKS

Best, W.M.,(1911).**The Principles of the Law of Evidence**. London: Sweet & Maxwell.

Heydon, J.D (1991) **Evidence**: Cases and Materials, 3rdEdn,

John Kaplan &Others.(1991), **Evidence Cases and Materials**, 7th Edition, Foundation Press, New York, USA.

Judiciary of Tanzania.,**A Handbook For Magistrates In The Primary Courts:**Published By The Judiciary of Tanzania With The Support of The World Bank, January,2019

M.N. Howard, et al (1990) **Phipson on Evidence**, 14thEdition

Mapunda B.T., (2004). **Evidence Part one, Two & Three**, 1st Ed., The Open University of Tanzania, Dar es Salaam

Morris, H.F (1968). **Evidence in East Africa**: Sweet & Maxwell, African University Press, Lagos, Nigeria.

Peter Murphy, (1992). **A practical Approach to Evidence.**4th Ed, Blackstone Press Ltd, London.

Phipson, S.L (1982) **Phipson on Evidence**

Ratanlal, R&D.K.Thakore (2004).**The Law of Evidence, 21st Edn**

Sarkar, M. C., (1983), **Sarkar's Law of Evidence**, 14thEdn.,Vol.1